Unique
CAPPADOCIA
"The Göreme region"

UĞUR AYYILDIZ
Art Historian and Professional Guide

NET ®
TURİSTİK YAYINLAR SANAYİ VE TİCARET A.Ş.

Cover photograph: Uçhisar, from the north.

Published and distributed by:
NET TURİSTİK YAYINLAR A.Ş.

Yerebatan Caddesi, 15/3,
34410 Cağaloğlu, İstanbul-Turkey
Tel: (90-1) 5208406-5274270
Telex: 23264 acı tr

1363. Sokak, 1, Kat.5,
35230 Çankaya, İzmir-Turkey
Tel: (90-51) 123001-253861

Deniz Mahallesi, 126. Sokak,
Çöllü Ap. D. 2-4, Antalya-Turkey
Tel: (90-31) 114314-173105

Yenimahalle, Çay Harkı Sokak,
5. Blok D. 1 Nevşehir-Turkey
Tel: (90-4851) 3089

Photograps: **Uğur Ayyıldız**
Layout: **Not Ajans**
Typesetting: **Sistem Foto Dizgi**
Colour Separation: **Işın Reprodüksiyon**
Printed in Turkey by: **Marşaş Matbaacılık A.Ş.**

ISBN 975-479-025-6

CONTENS

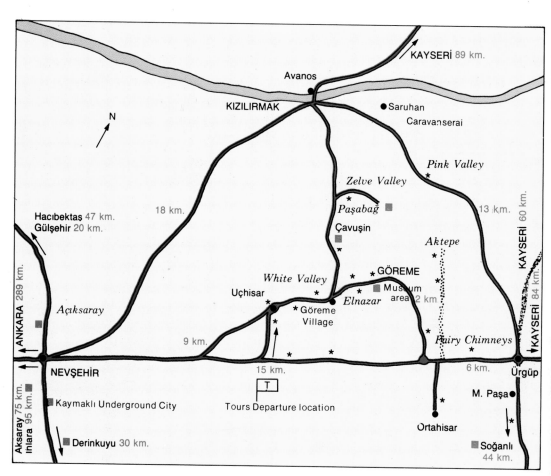

Touring map of Göreme and environs.
*Scenic view spots.

FOREWORD

Turkey, a country with a rich variety of attractions for the visitor, offers a tremendous treasure of historical and archeological sites, innumerable tumuli and unique scenery and still the «Göreme region» holds a distinguished position among them all. Situated in this region is the Göreme valley and a village by the same name (formerly called Avcılar).

Known as Cappadocia in ancient times, the Göreme region is located within a triangular area surrounded by the cities of Kayseri-Aksaray-Niğde. This territory also happens to be the geographical center of the Anatolian plains. Starting from the central plains and the Salt Lake, the land climbs in steps to higher altitudes towards the east. Natural routes that once crossed Anatolia, used to pass over or meet in Cappadocia. Vegetation in the environs is far from being abundant. It was mainly the crossroads and the watersides (the springs) that motivated inhabitation in the area. Today Nevşehir is the district center whereas the shopping center lies in Ürgüp.

The Symbol of the Göreme Region: The fairy chimneys to the west of Ürgüp.
The Erciyas mountain in the background.

TIPS FOR THE PHOTOGRAPHERS

The Göreme region is one of the most beautiful spots in the world. Nowhere else can one find such a variety of enchanting formations.

In order to take vivid photographs in this region, one should make the most of lights and shadows at the right time of the day. Shots from the high terraces of valleys below can be taken by shielding the lens (a.g. the environs of Uçhisar, the valley descending into Göreme village, El Nazar valley, etc.). These places offer better pictures in the forenoon hours, along the course of the tours. The famous fairy chimneys at the entrance to Ürgüp, the northern side of the Uçhisar formation, the Zelve valley and nearby formations can ideally be photographed in the late afternoon hours.

A flashlight is necessary to take photographs of frescoes within churches and in the underground cities. Before noon is the best time to capture the wide panoramic views available from the end of the shattered pathway going from Ortahisar to Aktepe or from the high spots in the environs and for the Açık Saray formations near Nevşehir with facades of imitation architectural structures.

Close shots of local people should not be attempted without permission. It is understandable that in one's private world of home garden and field, no one would like to be the target of cameras day after day. Either use your tele-lens or ask for permission.

Entrance into the Zelve valley: The Paşabağ location.

The Aktepe panoramic viewing spot: Kızılçukur.

INTRODUCTION

Besides its unequaled and striking scenery, Göreme is full of artistic products belonging to different civilizations. An active rural life, with all its authentic color and folklore, completes the atmosphere. Most of the monasteries, churches and monk cells are decorated with frescoes. Nature, history, art and life itself meet nowhere else in such harmony and unity. Once this magnificent sight was likened to the «surface of the moon». But now we know that such a view does not exist even on the moon.

The type of soil in the area is «tufa» which exhibits different colors in different parts. This diversity in color is due to the variety in the metallic nature of different volcanic eruptions. Although «tufa» is hard on the surface, it easily gives way to digging. With the addition of manure, it is highly productive in agriculture. Steep valley slopes, pyramidal and chimney shaped formations have been for ages easily digged for different purposes. The mystery in the atmosphere is completed by pointed rock formations called troglodites or «fairy chimneys». The fortress-like, big block formations are also hardened and accumulated natural formations. The best known is Uçhisar.

The northern part of the Göreme valley: Erosion is still effective even if considerably decelerated.

From late spring to late autumn hotels are nearly full. Most of the visitors to the region are organized groups which are touring Anatolia. There is a sufficient number of adequate camping areas in the neighborhood.

Possibilities for the night life are so called discos in the hotels or several carved caves, in which folkloric dancing groups perform shows.

There are several research and publications about the Göreme region prepared by some visitors; medical doctors, missioners men of different professions. They were all attracted with this fabulous region.

A French traveller Paul Lucas in 18th century was the earliest. Father G.de Jerphanion's publications was the first extensive work. (His studies from 1907 on were later published, the first volume in 1925 and the last in 1945; they consist of two volumes of text and three of photographs) Some of the mistakes of this publications, especially on dates had been repeated in later publications.

Some other books about the region were Thierry couple's Ihlara Valley published in 1963; Geerkon couple's «Göreme» published in 1968. An extensive and important research was prepared by a group of scholars and published in one large volume in 1971 by Nagel Publishers.

UNRIVALLED CAPPADOCIA

Formation:

No man has ever ventured to this day, to name the seven wonders of nature on this old earth.

Yet should there be such an attempt, the Göreme region would no doubt outshine most candidates and take its place on top of that list. The peculiar formations and sights of this region are definitely unique. One cannot help feeling that some majestic sorcerer has chosen this place to perform his magical wonders.

Everything started with the rise of several volcanoes around the area; for a long period of time they erupted and scattered their volcanic dust, ashes, lava and other remains over and around. Accumulated in the surrounding lakes and valleys, these volcanic residues then became prone to successive erosions through winds, rains and differences in temperature and started to take myriad forms.

Then came a series of earthquakes, and the Göreme region inclined towards the Kızılırmak (the Red River) valley, which increased the impact of erosion. Although the pace of erosion has slowed down lately by comparison it can still be observed today.

This geological process has, in fact, occurred quite recently. Split into a considerable number of valleys, the Göreme region covers a wide area. Its southern boundary is lined with the hills of table-shaped mountains and between them lies the Soğanlı valley, adorned with a variety of formations. To the west, on the slopes of the Hasan mountain, the Ihlara valley twists and extends as a deep canyon. Unlike the others in appearance, with great blocks tumbled down from the peaks, Ihlara valley shelters a great number of churches and monastery rooms carved into the rocks.

Typical examples of the early formations can be seen along the main road of Nevşehir-Ürgüp. From the upper tip of the plateau on this end, down towards the drainage valley of Kızılırmak, are a row of valleys, carved by the torrent waters. Separated from the slopes of the valleys, there are many examples of «fairy chimneys», as they are quite accurately and imaginatively called, pyramidal, pointed and conical in shape, with protective caps on their tops. There are other typical examples in the entrances to the Ürgüp and Zelve valleys. Their pink, beige-grey, yellow, grey, white and other colors reveal different tones at different hours of the day.

The highest peak in the region is the Erciyas volcano, 3917 m. in altitude, with its fantastic conical silhouette in the east, and the Hasan mountain in the west is 3263 m. in altitude. The Melendiz mountains are located in between.

The Hasandağ and Erciyes volcanos.

The severity of erosion manifests itself in different ways on the hills and in the valleys. In the photograph, the north of Zelve, the silhouette of the fairy chimneys in front of the white slope.

The entrance of a valley extending from the Nevşehir-Ürgüp main road to the drainage valley of the Kızılırmak river. In the background, the Uçhisar formation

While the bottoms of valleys were used as small fields or vineyards, available slopes have always been open to settlements during all periods.

The bottoms of valleys are crowded here and there with pyramidal shaped formations. The west of the village of Göreme.

HISTORY

The rich soil of Anatolia has a distinguished standing in the archeological world. From the first man to our day, Asia Minor has sheltered such a variety and wealth of civilizations as can be seen nowhere else. Although only a limited number of objects dating back to antiquity have been found in the area, its geographical position gives us every reason to believe that it has been inhabited since very early times. The Anatolian neolithic habitation center Çatalhöyük is only a bird's fly away, 200 km. from the region. A wall fresco in Çatalhöyük, the first city settlement and an extraordinarily highly developed civilization center founded in the 7th Millenium B.C., shows the drawing of the twin capped Hasandağı volcano in eruption. It is interesting that the western volcano of Cappadocia appears in this fresco, which is accepted to be the first pastoral painting. Just beside the Erciyas mountain, which is the eastern volcano of the region, lies Kültepe (early 2nd Millenium B.C.), a site of the Hittites, the first empire of Anatolia. The Kızılırmak River, the vital artery of this empire, crosses Cappadocia from one end to the other.

The excavations of Karahöyük in Hacıbektas town and Acemhöyük on the plain near Aksaray, from the Early Bronze age are still going on.

Anatolia is a natural bridge binding Asia to Europe. This part of the world for ages has been the target of many an invasion, coming from the east or the west. Cappadocia has functioned at all these times of turmoil as a shelter to Anatolian people seeking refuge. Remnants of many a tribe found lodging for long periods in these hidden shelters, even underground cities, dug into those mysterious formations which aroused fear in hostile forces that set eyes upon them.

The earliest literature which mentions the region and Eastern Anatolia is Xenefon's **Anabasis,** dating back to 401 B.C. Those were the times when this area, in contrast to seaside settlements, could stay immune to outside forces. Alexander the Great took the region under his rule, and following him, the states established by his generals kept the area under control. The region was governed by local Cappadocian princes, supported by these states, until the Roman invasion in 17 A.D. These princes had gained wide fame with their thoroughbred horses.

The entrance into an untitled church. The museum grounds, Göreme.

The Roman eagle on the peak: the bronze symbol of the Roman sovereignty. (From the private collection of the author.)

Bronze bathing tub: Roman period, Kayseri museum.

BYZANTINE AND TURKISH ERA

There is no sign of a monastic way of life in Anatolia during the early Christian period.

However in Egypt (Thebaid) and in the Holy Land the monastic way of life was adopted by a great many people. After Islamic Arabs conquered these areas, many Christian groups took refuge in the interior of Anatolia and continued their monastic way of life in accordance with their religious beliefs. It was the 7th century that witnessed these events. In Binbir Kilise (1001 Church) on the Toros mountains in the south, in Heraklia (near Miletus) on Bafa Lake (Aegean region), in Uludağ in Bursa, and finally in the Cappadocian region there was an outgrowth of extensive monastery life. In Cappadocia's Göreme and Ihlara valleys, church frescoes and decorations and architectural designs of churches show a definite blend of Egyptian, Syrian and Anatolian influences in planning and style. It is therefore a pity that of the great number of castles, churches and monasteries that were built in the 7th - 9th centuries, the ruins of only one or two could survive to our day. In the 7th century it was mentioned in the Acts of local Saint Hieron that some christians are living in the caves of «Koroma».

The mosaic and fresco art of the Byzantine Empire reserves certain parts of churches for Biblical themes, according to certain principles. These frescoes were produced by the artists in the capital whereas in the provinces, it was the monks who practised the art. Understandably, the majority of the Cappadocian church frescoes reflect the comparatively primitive provincial style.

The Cappadocian churches had to obey the rules of the icon prohibition period (Iconoclastic era) during the years 726-842. In rock churches in the Göreme region, simple forms and cross motifs can be seen on naked walls or under deteriorating fresco plasters. Some claim that these motifs belong to the iconoclastic period, but they do not.

It is quite clear that these churches dug into rocks were built according to the principles of the fashion of their day. Many of the columned churches in the Göreme region are four columned and cruciform, a style which appeared in the capital Istanbul in the 10th - 11th centuries. So churches built according to this plan spread from the capital to the provinces in the 11th and 12th centuries, when the Empire was at its peak in rule and artistic activity. The use of these plans in a rather uncreative, religious community such as Cappadocia could only come during this period and not earlier. Simple motifs which decorate the walls of some churches must have been drawn by monks as simple decorations, who knew that they would soon be covered by frescoes. In short, it is clear that the walls of churches carved into rocks according to a plan that originated well after the iconoclastic era cannot be decorated with motifs belonging to the iconoclastic period.

Tiny earthen jugs: (Monza Bulbs), used for carrying the sacred water from Jarusalem. Byzantine period. (From the author's private collection).

Relief from an earthen vase: Jesus Christ, local artwork.

The Ağzıkarahan Caravanserai: 13th century Seljuk. The kiosk mosque in the courtyard, view from the entrance.

Mausoleum of Hüdavent Khatun: Early 14th century, Niğde.

At the end of the 11th century, a great part of Anatolia came under the rule of the Seljuk Turks. Christians cherished a wide freedom under the tolerant Turkish governments. Some of the Cappadocian churches were built and frescoed during this Turkish period. It was the Mongolian invasion of the 13th. century that finally struck and hindered these activities.

One of the most important national and religious institutions established during the spread of Turkish influence in Anatolia was in the small village Hacı Bektaş in Cappadocia. Like the mausoleum of Hacı Bektaş, one time prominent Turkish thinker, a great many other mausoleums, mosques, and others are classical Seljuk and Ottoman art works that reach our day. The main route that ,passing through Cappadocia, ties the Seljuk capital Konya to districts Kayseri and Sivas is lined with a row of caravanserais which are unique, strictly Turkish in creation. The caravanserais were a series of motels or inns, built in the form of a castle and were especially influential in encouraging travelling and commerce. The Christian villages of those times survived side by side with their Turkish neighbors up until the 1920's. They were discharged then, according to an immigrant exchange agreement signed by the Greek and the Turkish governments.

A great number of frescoes carry the inscription of a Christian name and a date beside them. It so happened that the later Christians believed in the miraculous medicinal effect of drinking the broken pieces of these frescoes added to water. Such ignorant and destructive misuses by the local people and the tourists have since been stopped and all important buildings in the area have been put under the protection of the local museum directorate.

The western façade of Uçhisar: Cavities served a multitude of purposes at different times.

East of Uçhisar: Twin capped fairy chimney. The interior is carved into several storeys to be used as monk cells.

ROCK SETTLEMENTS

Simple, single-naved, vaulted churches constitute the earliest of the Cappadocian churches, presumably dating from the 7th - 8th centuries. The remaining ones, the columns, domes and other architectural elements of which are also carved into the rocks are later, from the 11th - 13th centuries. The doors and windows of monasteries, dormitories, dining rooms, monk cells and most of the churches cannot be spotted from the outside. They have been dug in such a way that no enemy could easily reach them. The openings observed today were caused by later collapses. Narrow and difficult entrances or passages have been equipped with round doors carved in the form of millstones out of nearby rocks. Ventilation chimneys and windows were all concealed.

There were about 10 underground cities in the region. Two of them, Derinkuyu and Kaymaklı are open to visitors today. These underground cities which go down meters-deep to 7-8 stories with small and large rooms, halls, churches and ventilation chimneys must have been dug by different tribes of people in different times. Rock settlements are in fact scattered in a much wider area than can be visited today. There are, for example, similar settlements in the north, near Kırşehir.

The bottoms of deep valleys are narrow and restricted, but marshy and therefore suitable for agriculture. The slopes on the other hand, are ideal for rock-carved habitation.

Pigeon manure means fertility for tufa, the local soil. Even today, as in the olden days, villagers show careful attention to private dovecots. Some valley slopes are filled with many small niches. These are old dovecots with their fallen-off facades.

The Eastern Christian tradition of monasticism advocates an isolated life style for all members of the family and the commune. As an isolated locality itself, Cappadocia was exceptionally suitable for such a mystique and for a relatively safe communal life. It possesses small valleys and wide grounds on plateaus which easily offer lodging to a limited population. A large number of child graves are evidence for the crowded family groups which lived here. On the other hand, there are a great number of small, single monk cells carved into the fairy chimneys, to live in as the way of the famous Syrian saint Simeon Stylite. The best known of these innumerable monastic centers scattered over the valleys is Göreme which was originally named Korama.

Göreme's monasteries and churches are located on an amphitheater-like slope and widely visited today within the museum grounds.

The method of rock carving used in those days is today called «cut». Relatively simple digging equipment is used for the purpose. Spaces carved into these rocks are extraordinarily fit for living and storing. They are humid all through the year and no insects can live in them. They are used even today as living spaces, motels, warehouses and stables and some (recently cut) are used as storehouses for the seasonal preservation of lemons, oranges and apples.

Pigeon flocks resting around nets.

An old dwelling used nowdays as a motel.

Pre christian era rock temple or grave, in Göreme village.

East of Ürgüp, St. Theodorus Church in Yeşilöz village. The largest and the only church with a gallery in the area (11th century).

Cells from monasteries, chapels and monk cells, visible through their fallen down façades, Zelve.

Stone blocks cut out of hardened tufa have been used at every period. The massive blocks are delivered from nearby quarries, where they are shaped by master craftsmen.

SIGHTSEEING TOURS

The largest district in the area is Kayseri, and Göreme lies at a distance of 100 km. from the Kayseri airport. An alternative way of reaching the region is by the Ankara-Nevşehir route which is 300 km. long. There is, in fact, regular bus transportation from all of the major cities of the country. Individual visitors can easily find experienced guides and drivers in the region.

All roads are in good condition and satisfactory motels and pension-houses are easy to find. The travelling season starts in April and continues up until the end of November. The winters in Göreme are rather cold, but strikingly beautiful. The climate is continental, summer days are warm and nights rather chilly. The altitude in Nevşehir is 1194 m. Autumn is long, sparkling and is the most colorful season here. Apricot and poplar, the characteristic trees of the region, display a rich color scheme with their yellow, red and green leaves under clear blue skies. Local produce includes potatoes, onions and beans. Villages and fields in sowing and harvesting seasons, and marketplaces on regular days are crowded with colorful local people. Villagers use horse carriages and donkeys for transportation. The hair tresses of the young village girls is a traditional and fashionable head-dress dating from the Hittite era.

The major handicraft of the region is carpetry. Dried apricots and delicious wines are, also, characteristic.

Bus tours visit only those places along the general tourist route. Although individual cars can reach some locations in the interior, a thorough, visit of the locality is only possible by foot and in a couple of days. Regulated tours cover all the «must» spectacles.

Tours depart from Nevşehir, Ürgüp, or Avanos and other centers and follow the main road of Nevşehir-Ürgüp and enter the region from Uçhisar, to provide a general view of the total formation and the peculiar light effects. Present day roads, careful not to harm the wonderland, pass between the vineyards that grow on ideal tufa soil and from which come the famous local wines.

Folklore group of the region during a show.

Fairy chimneys west of Ürgüp.

A headdress, fashionable since the days of the Hittites.

Kayseri is a leading centre in handwoven carpets, which are produced in great many homes in Ürgüp and in its environs.

Although there are wide fields in the surroundings of Göreme, agriculture is carried out even on the smallest piece of land. Traditional tools, cheaper and more practical, are preferred to the modern ones.

Nature, history and daily life intermingle in perfect harmony in the region.

Colourful carts are the rural vehicles of families, working collectively in the fields during sowing and harvesting months.

Turkey is a heaven of fruit and vegetables. Species rare in Göreme are brought in from other provinces, especially from the Mediterranean region.

Home economics of the region includes preservation of fruits and vegetables for winter, by either boiling or drying local produces.

UÇHİSAR

At the tip of the high plateau, Uçhisar looks like a majestic fortress, with myriad holes and openings on its facade, which are due to former collapses. Just outside the small town, situated on the out skirts of the fortress, is a picturesque little rock motel. There is an extraordinary view from the ridge just behind this motel, with an outstanding panorama right at one's feet. Yellow, pink and grey valley slopes are full of dovecots with their tiny windows. The foot of the valley extends in wide bends. To the north of Uçhisar, there is another striking view. The majestic fortress, the fairy chimneys, small settlements and valley alltogether bewitch the spectator.

Yet one has to revisit this locality in the late afternoon, in order to catch the ideal light for photographs.

Uçhisar founded at the skirts of the fortress, on a dominant spot overlooking the Göreme view. Below lies the valley of Kızılırmak.

Dovecot formations, on the banks of the valley, extenting downhill from the east of Uçhisar, are visible from across the motel carved into the rocks. Manure is collected at regular intervals.

Western façade of Uçhisar.

The panaromic viewing spot, resembling a terrace, in between Uçhisar and the village of Göreme. Below, the village of Göreme is visible among fairy chimneys, and Aktepe in the background.

Scenic Views

Following the pause in Uçhisar, the tours descend into the Göreme village. At the right of this road after a short walk, one reaches a panoramic spot with an unequaled view, which no words can accurately describe and to which no photographs can do justice. The chief cause of all these formations, the Erciyas volcano, rises in all its grandeur in the east, as can be observed from the other platforms in the region.

A short distance away, on the left side of the road descending into Göreme, lies the «snow white» canyon of the region. The narrow canyon starts from Uçhisar, deepens suddenly and opens to the Kızılırmak valley.

The bottoms of these valleys and every single available piece of land on their banks are cultivated.

As cars reach the plain below, the lower wide brim of the valley in view since leaving Uçhisar can be seen. Now one can begin to spot a few churches carved into the fairy chimneys.

First Maçan - Avcılar, and then the typical Cappadocian village Göreme, as it is called today, appear at last. Today some of the old houses caved into rock pyramids are used as restaurants and some as motels. On the village square, there is a rock cut temple or mausoleum surviving from the pre-Christian period, with its columns in the front and the lower part of it broken down. Many of the houses here, as those situated in the whole neighborhood, are built from tufa stones. There is traffic of horse carriages and donkeys, and the village coffeehouse is crowded with visitors and, in off-season, menfolk of the villages. On the inner bank, there is a beautiful old mansion house.

$\longrightarrow$

Valley on the Nevşehir-Ürgüp highway

There are small fields among fairy chimneys in the valley extending between Uçhisar and Göreme.

Varied formations on the bank of the same valley.

Interesting formations are situated at the spot where the slope meets the foot of the valley.

The White valley: Also called the "Snow white valley", this formation starts from the northeastern end of Uçhisar, forming two valleys which meet in a deep canyon below.

The White valley: There are small fields on the narrow ridge between canyons.

Starting from the meeting spot of the canyons, the valley, expanding with twists, extends into the distance.

Reaching the village of Göreme from Uçhisar, one comes across to chapels and monasteries carved into fairy chimneys. The first fairy chimney here was a grave chapel.

Down into the valley, the big fairy chimneys were dug to be used as monasteries, and some have graves.

The village of Göreme is a typical, old habitation centre of the region. The houses are built out of local tufa stone blocks. An early period temple or grave dug into a rock, the houses and a motel are the main attractions in the village. (See p. 18)

GÖREME VALLEY

Near Göreme village one comes to the museum ground where the «Göreme churches and the monasteries» are located. The Elnazar valley and the Saklı Church (The Hidden Church), which are not usually visited by the regular tours, are situated to the right of this road and can only be reached by a narrow pathway. The frescoes of the Hidden Church have survived intact for centuries, because the entrance of the church stayed hidden due to a collapse. Dozen of fairy chimneys, in various shapes and sizes are lined all across the Elnazar valley. One of the larger ones has been transformed into a rock church and decorated with frescoes. As one climbs up to the museum from the main road, on the left slope, one sees the Church of the Virgin Mary, and behind this ridge extends the magnificent Kılıçlar Valley (The Swords Valley). The four-columned Kılıçlar Church, which is very simply decorated with no frescoes, lies here.

The Elnazar valley lies to the east of the village of Göreme. The valley is reached with a narrow pathway, to the right of road, leading to the museum grounds.

The Kılıçlar Valley is on the other side of the hills to the left on the road leading to the museum area.

The Tokalı Church, beside the parking lot, to the left of the road leading from the village of Göreme to the museum area. The fairy chimney down the road was a monk cell.

Below: There is a viewing spot on the hills above the Tokalı Church overlooking Aktepe. The Church of Virgin Mary, decorated with frescoes also lies on this ridge.

TOKALI CHURCH

The Tokalı Church (The Buckled Church), the largest in the neighborhood, can be seen on the left, a couple of hundred meters from the parking lot of the Göreme Museum area. The arched entrance hall is known as the old church, whereas the wider inner one, vaulted and naved, is known as the new church. The frescoes of the older church are from the early 10th century, primitive and provincial in style; those of the new church belong to the late 10th century, in the rare capital style. The frescoes found here are highly artistic and unique in the region with their dominating blue color and «iconographic» characteristics. The main and side apses and arch peers give a certain majestic appearance to the church.

The Tokalı Church: Entrance leads through the small hall into the large, vaulted church interior. It rises over an apse façade and two side wall piers and arches. The frescoes are lined in friezes.

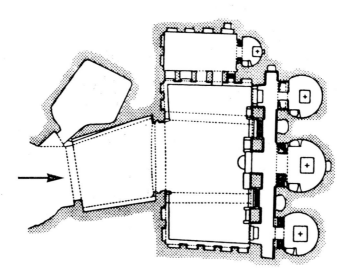

The plan of the Tokalı Church.

The fresco of Jesus and the Apostles.

Behind the museum building rises the rock mass which contains the "Kızlar monastery. The churches around here are connected with pathways.

CHURCHES WITHIN THE MUSEUM AREA

Entering the museum, monasteries scattered on the right and the left begin to come into sight. (It should be noted that the names given to churches in this whole region are local adaptions, and not the original names.)

The churches are carved in accordance with the natural formations and availability of the blocks of rocks. For this reason, the entrances and apses of each church face different directions. The columns, apses, roofs, vaults and domes have all been dug into rocks. The frescoes on the walls are traced back to the 11th or 12 th centuries. Decorations look alike, but there is a difference in color tones. The themes of the frescoes reflect significant Christian festivities advocated by the Church. The names of subjects and people are inscribed beside the figures. Themes from the life of Jesus Christ are represented in the lage panels. Inside the arches and on the peers, there are the pictures of the saints in busts, or within full size.

The deep valley and the slope containing dovecots with deteriorating facades are seen across from the entrance, beside the modern fountain in the shape of a fairy chimney. The first church in this locality is unnamed; passing through the narthex lined with small and large graves, one enters the vaulted church through arched doors. There are some frescoes drawn on the unplastered wall. **(Plan No: 1, see page 42)**

The panoramic sight of the museum grounds: The "Kızlar" monastery in the centre, the Karanlık Church on the right bank.

Göreme open air museum: The positions and plans of churches. The numbers are ascribed according to the order followed during tours.

1- The Unnamed Church
2- The Elmalı Church
3- The Church of Saint Barbara
4- The Yılanlı Church

5-6- Dining rooms and chambers, on the slope
7- The Karanlık Church
8- The Unnamed Church
9- The Çarıklı Church
10- The Kızlar Monastery

Entering the museum grounds, the "Kızlar" monastery lies to the left. (The rock block in the middle.) Behind it is the Monk's monastery. These are large complexes consisting of chambers, storage rooms, dining room and a church. Some of the divisions, connected with narrow passages or corridors are equipped with wheel doors.

THE ELMALI CHURCH (The Apple Church)
(Plan No: 2)

One enters the inner court through a narrow corridor and proceeds through the narrow gateway, into the church. It is domed, four columned and built with all its architectural elements within a square shaped, cruciform space, carved into the rock. Its window, opening out to the valley, illuminates the interior. From under the deteriorating frescoes, geometrical and cross motifs, painted on the walls, are seein here and there. The Deesis scene (Mary, John the Baptist and Jesus on the throne) is situated on the main apse. In the main dome is Christ Pantocrator and in the second smaller dome the fresco of the Archangel Gabriel. Better preserved frescoes are of the baptism and crucifixion of Jesus. On the arches the figures represent royal persons and/or church elders.

The Elmalı Church (11th C.): The apse. The left pillar is original, the right one is renewed during restorations.

The Elmalı Church: The entrance door, the columns, the apse and the domes, all have been formed by digging the rocks. On the walls, simple, uni-coloured decoration are visible from under the fallen off frescoes.

Central dome: The fresco of Jesus, the Pantocrator.

45

The fresco inside the small dome of the Elmalı Church shows the archangel holding a globe.

On the wall across the entrance, the Crucufixion of Jesus Christ. Inside the voult, there are the figures of prominenrt church personalities.

On the slope across the valley of the Churches of Elmalı and Saint barbara, there are dovecots with fallen down facades, exposing the nests inside.

THE CHURCH OF SAINT BARBARA

(Plan No: 3)

This church is located on the back side of the rock in which the Apple Church is situated. It is carved out of the rock with 2 columns, and the remaining 2 columns, as suggested by the cruciform plan, are subsitituted by the corners which have been left peered. The domes and 3 apses with the altars inside are intact.

It is adorned with simple decorations, drawn right on to the walls. One of the frescoes across the entrance, is of St. Barbara. Among the simple decorations, the three crosses above the right apse are interesting. The one in the middle, in double circles represents Jesus, while the ones on both sides refer to the two thieves who were crucified on the same day as Jesus. Four small circles beside the middle cross which represents Jesus, suggest Jesus' four wounds.

Because of its primitive, simple decorations this church is given as an example of the Iconoclastic period by some sources. As explained before, it can not be, but belongs to a later, 11th century period. **(See page 14)**

47

The Church of Saint Barbara is adorned with simple, original decorations, painted straight on to the walls.
Left: St. Theodoros and George, Right; on the side apse, cross drawings, representing Jesus Christ and the "Good Thieves"
Below: On the apse, the figure of Jesus Christ.

The Yılanlı Church (11th C.). The scene of St. George and Theodoros with the Dragon. These two saints had a certain eminence among the soldier saints.

THE YILANLI CHURCH (The Snake Church)
(Plan No : 4)

This is a vaulted, small burial chapel. The apse is on the left wall. On it can be seen St. George and St. Theodoros killing the Dragon. The figures on the side belong to Emperor Constantine the Great and his mother Helena. They hold the «true cross» in their hands. The halos on their heads are signs of their saintliness. There are three saint frescoes on the wall across the vault. The naked figure belongs to a wicked woman, who was changed to a man named Onouphirius. The upper ridge of the Snake Church is filled with many caved-in rooms and dining halls. **(Plan No : 5 and 6)**

Dining rooms and chambers, on the slope situated between the Yılanlı and the Karanlık Churches.

On the vault of the Yılanlı Church, to the left: Raised to the rank of sainthood, the Emperor Constantin the Great and his mother Helena, holding the true cross in their hands.

The section containing the Karanlık Church and its monastery. The interior spaces are visible because of the fallen façade. The small window below left is the only window of the church.

THE KARANLİK CHURCH (The Dark Church)

(Plan No: 7)

This is a complex of rooms. On the lower story is a dining hall (refectory) and on the upper a dormitory, the facade of which has fallen down. Through the narrow entrance, one climbs up several steps into the narthex of the Dark Church. It is a classical example of the four-columned, cruciform, domed type. It has a small window to the outside. Due to the lack of daylight, the colours of the frescoes have stayed very vivid. Jesus on the dome, the birth of Jesus on the left-hand wall and the transfiguration above the entrance are quite well preserved typical examples. The frescoe showing the ascension of Jesus on the narthex vault is unique. These frescoes are highly artistic products in the «capital style» and differ from the ones in other churches in the neighborhood.

In the lower part of the rock in which the Dark Church is situated, a nameless, columned church is located. The apse of this church has a separator, which distinguishes it from the other churches, the separators of which have collapsed in time. This separator (Iconostasis) is carved out of rock and is three- arched. The cross composed of 5 circles on the left side wall of the entrance is unique in the region. **(Plan No : 8)**

51

The rock mass which withholds the complex of the Karanlık Church. In spring the meadows are filled with tiny and colourful wild flowers.

The Karanlık Church dome: The fresco of Jesus Christ, the Pantocrator.

On the entrance hall vault of the Karanlık Church, Jesus Christ raised to the sky by the angels: The frescoes of the church are in good condition and in "capital" style.

The fresco of the Birth of Jesus Christ.

The decorative pattern advised by the Church is fully achieved in the Karanlık Church. John the Baptist baptizing Jesus Christ in a schematic river.

Jesus Christ crucified.

THE ÇARIKLI CHURCH (The Sandaled Church)

(Plan No : 9)

This one is domed, cruciform in shape with 2 columns and 2 peered corner walls. It receives sufficient light from the entrance which contains a modern stairway. The themes of its frescoes are similar to those of the others, but have been badly harmed. The church derives its name from the footsteps inscribed on the floor.

On the slope rising between the Karanlık and the Çarıklı Church, there is an untitled church, its features all in good condition, but without any frescoes. There is an interesting cross motif made up of five circles on the left wall in its entrance hall. (Plan No: 8)

The Old Çavuşin: The light coloured wall seen below the protruding section resembling a roof fringe, is the pillared entrance of the famous Basilica of John the Baptist, which has collapsed quite recently.

ÇAVUŞİN

On the right-hand side of the road going down to Avanos and the Kızılırmak valley from the village of Göreme is the Çavuşin village. A high, concave-shaped slope, its facade filled with holes, meets the eye immediately. After the collapse of this slope, the former Çavuşin village was rebuilt on the plain. Once, the Church of John the Baptist in this locality was 3-naved and its facade reflected the Syrian influence. According to some sources, it was the oldest (8th. C.) church of the region. Its facade fell down because of erosion in recent times. On the side of the road, on the slope outside the lower end of the village, there is the small, vault roofed Çavuşin Church (Nicephorus Phocas Church). Its frescoes drawn in chapters as a pictured story are dated from the second half on the 10th century.

57

ZELVE

The Çavuşin-Avanos road turns to Zelve from beside a couple of fairy chimneys which rise in front of a high slope, as if to salute the passers-by.

One of the most interesting formations of fairy chimneys in the region can be found here. The «Paşabağ» locality, a couple of kilometres before the Zelve valley, has twin, triplet and other fairy chimneys offering a beautiful opportunity for photographers, especially in the afternoon hours. The pyramidal rock formations that rise from among the vineyards, apple and apricot orchards, are characteristic examples of «Cappadocian formation».

Zelve consists of two canyons, extending side by side in a narrow, deep valley. This spot is the pink realm of the region. Just beside the museum entrance, there is an oasis-like, cool picnic ground under the century-old trees. The whiteness of the left bank complements the pink color of the valley and the right bank. The Zelve village, once located in the valley, was moved in the 1950's to the nearer plain, due to the threat of erosion. Some of the valley slopes are filled with holes and openings caused by collapses.

The sole witnesses of the old settlement in this locality today is a small mosque, with a bell tower-shaped minaret.

The road to Zelve passes by the fairy chimneys in the Paşabağ locality. The effects of erosion are perfectly visible here.

Minaret of the abandoned village of Zelve Valley.

The Paşabağ locality on the Zelve road.

Rising by the road, the fairy chimney, the interior of which is dug to be used as either a chapel or a cell.

Entering the Zelve valley: The inner valley is divided into two by a narrow, wall-like seperator and extends down into the distance. The valley on the right was once the habitation area of the old Zelve village.

Two large cavities at the bottom of the valley.

Formations of the Zelve valley.

The handmade pots and pans.

AVANOS

Avanos is a charming little village situated on the skirts of high hills, north of the Göreme area.

Anatolia's longest river Kızılırmak (the antique Halyas) crosses the village. The typical Avanos village attracts attention with its old houses, settlement styles, 2 middle-class hotels and its red earthenware pots and jugs the colour of which comes from the earth of this district.

The Turkish hand-woven carpet production and sale centre located of the entrance of Avanos is the biggest and most modern complex of the district.

Another speciality of Avanos are the qualified onyx vases and orna. of different colours and styles. The used onyx is found here. The Saruhan Kervansarayı (Saruhan Caravanserai) situated on the east part of Avanos is a fine example of the 13th century Seljuk architecture.

A pottery workshop in Avanos.

ÜRGÜP

Along the road from Avanos to Ürgüp, there are pink formations and tufa stone quarries which supply the material used in the building of the local houses. By the Nevşehir-Ürgüp road, fairy chimneys line the approach.

Famous for its wines, Ürgüp is located on a fortress-like slope rising from the plain at its foot.

Ürgüp is the shopping center of the Göreme region, encompassing the first tourist hotel of the area, a recently built large motel complex, many pension houses, a marketplace, banks and a museum.

At 20 kilometres from Ürgüp, on a narrow village road that turns off from the main route to Kayseri is located the largest rock church of the Cappadocian region, the Tagar church. It is a four-columned, domed church with a gallery lining its upper story. Having been dedicated to «St. Theodore», the frescoes of the church belong to the 11th - 13th centuries. It receives light from the dome, which has partly fallen down. It is the only rock church of the region with a gallery. **(For picture see p.18)**

Just beside the fairy chimneys, symbols of the region, a youngster preparing souvenir statuettes out of local stone, typical of this region.

The new Ürgüp motel foundations on the Nevşehir exit. It was inspired by the typical town housings.

ORTAHİSAR

On both sides of the road entering the town, there are a great number of old and new storehouses carved out of the rocks. Locally produced potatoes and apples, and lemons and oranges brought in from the Mediterranean region are kept here in cool storages for long periods of time. A small town, Ortahisar has developed around a fortress-like, big block formation. The fortress is an «all times» settlement with its holes and openings on the facade, due to successive collapses.

A building complex with an eiwan is situated 1 km northeast of Ortahisar. The locally called Hallaç Manastırı is a monastery complex carved into the rocks and a fine example of its type due to its 3 sides, each being a church of a different style. One side is open.

As one comes out of Ortahisar on to the Ürgüp-Nevşehir road, there is a pathway twisting away and going up to Aktepe just in front. At the end of this road, there is one of the most beautiful sights in the Göreme region. In the west there is a panoramic spot which looks on to a wide vista, starting from the Kızıl Çukur (red cavity), covering Çavuşin and Elnazar valley and reaching out to Uçhisar on the horizon. The best time to take pictures here, on clear days, is before noon.

On the Ortahisar town square, the fortress-like formation from which the town derives its name.

The Aktepe viewing spot, at the end of the pathway across the road which connects Ortahisar to the main route.

Aktepe slope formations.

The view to the west from Aktepe: Kızılçukur in the foreground, the Elnazar valley and the village of Göreme in the centre, and Uçhisar above.

Snow-covered top of Erciyes mountain seen from the Ürgüp-Soğanlı highway.

SOĞANLI

The Ürgüp-Soğanlı road, passing through various typical «Göreme» sights and crossing over beyond the hills and the interiors of valleys, extends far into the distance. Mustafa Paşa (Sinosos) village is 6 km. away from Ürgüp.

There are a variety of formations in the Soğanlı valley, which is located on the southern end of Göreme, between a series of table-shaped mountains. There are a great number of churches and monasteries in the valley and on the banks. Most of them are decorated with frescoes. On the slope of the valley, the «Domed Church», the exterior and the dome of which are carved out of tufa, is the symbol of this area. The slopes of the valley are filled with innumerable small windows painted white. These are the dovecots, from which manure is obtained by the villagers for agriculture.

The most famous of the churches is the Karabaş church with an inscription dated 1060-61. The Communion of the Twelve Apostles fresco is a masterpiece in «capital style.»

The Soğanlı valley: It is situated among table shaped flat hills. The "Domed Church" in the centre.

Fresco of the forty martyrs of Suvasa (11th century).

The frescoes of the Karabaş Church in the Soğanlı Valley are works of high artistic quality. (11th C.)
In detail photograph: Virgin Mary with Christ Child in the temple.

Typical dovecots, peculiar to the Soğanlı valley.
The entrance holes are painted in white for distracting the attention of birds.

NEVŞEHİR

Nevşehir, a settlement since the Hittite era, is located on the outskirts of a hill where an Ottoman castle is situated. The Kurşunlu Mosque, built in the 19th century by Damat İbrahim Pasha is a beautiful example of Turkish architecture. The theological school built in the same century is ştill used for various purposes like hospice and library.

Nevşehir, the province centre of the Göreme area, has a couple of middle-class hotels. There are regular bus lines from all important centres of Turkey to Nevşehir.

Nevşehir and Ürgüp are the starting point of daily excursion tours organized in the area.

The Açık Saray (Open Palace), a rock carved settlement on the Gülşehir-Hacıbektaş road is an interesting spot. The villages scattered on the valley slops on the way to Kaymaklı from Nevşehir, exhibit the district's typical pictorial village types with their houses and settlement style. Nevşehir also possesses an archaeological museum containing the area's unearthed archaeological findings.

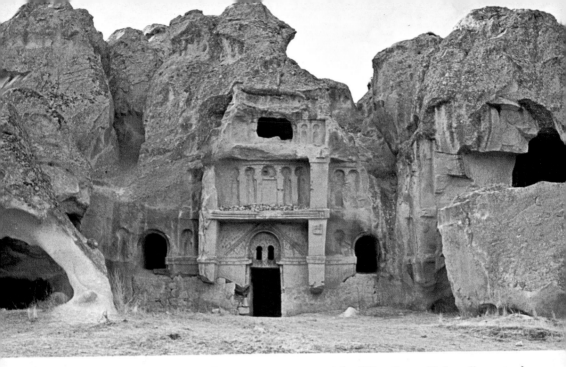

North of Nevşehir, by the road leading to Gülşehir, "The Open Palace", one of the churches with façades resembling architectural structures.

"The Open Palace" has no frescoes. Some walls, ceilings and niches are decorated with cross motifs.

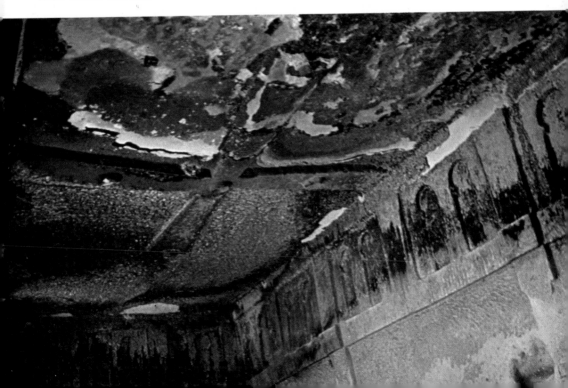

Erosion has created some very interesting formations in "The Open Palace" area.

KAYMAKLI Underground City

Kaymaklı is a small town 20 km. to the south of Nevşehir. Right through the slope of a low hill, just in the center, one enters the largest underground city of the region. The eight-storied underground city is today rearranged, illuminated, and provided with precautionary measures for the safety of visitors. This, like the other underground cities in the neighborhood, was designed and built by the efforts of many generations of people, to be used as shelter against all kinds of threats and invasions in the pre-Christion as well as the Christian periods. Fresh air was supplied by systems of ventilation chimneys to these self-sufficient, relatively safe sheltering grounds. The stories were connected by narrow passages and separated by mill-stone-like, round safety doors. The storage cavities for amphoras, the round doors, the rooms, the basilica, the meeting room and the graves are all of major interest.

The third floor of the Kaymaklı underground city: The underground cities are quite cool. It is wise to be cautious during excursions.

Amphora and earthenware in a niche at the entrance of a ruin

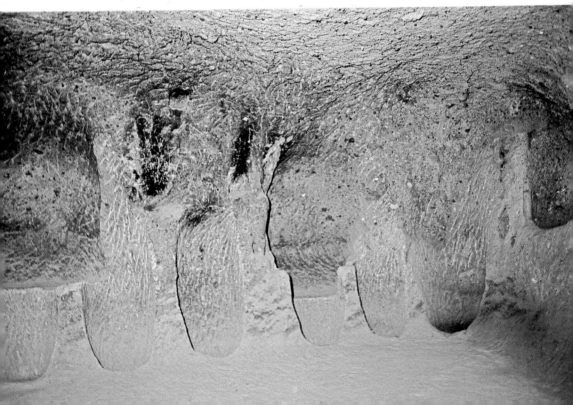

Cross sectional sketch of the Kaymaklı underground city.
Below: Living cells lined around a hall and the passageway leading to the lower floor at the far end. The collapsed sections between floors are reinforced and tour areas are lighted up.

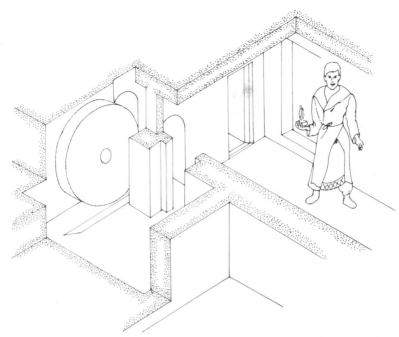

The Kaymaklı underground city divisions, passage and wheel doors.

Wheel doors, shaped in place, closing certain parts of passages by blocking the way.

The basilica of the Kaymaklı underground city: It has two apses, with an altar in te centre.

The largest hall of the underground city, reserved as a restroom for the visitors. Living spaces are situated aronud it and there is a pier in its centre. It is connected to the lower and upper storeys with narrow passages.

The church built in the town of Derinkuyu in the recent periods.

DERİNKUYU Underground City

Derinkuyu is another underground city located 10 km. to the south of Kaymaklı. Until recently there were a number of basements, storage rooms and deep water wells under the houses in this town. Some happy coincidences and investigations that followed, identified these rooms as the parts of a large underground city.

Derinkuyu has a distinguished place among the many well-known underground cities in the region. Some Hittite works and «The Eagle on the Summit» statues symbolizing the victory of the Roman conquest were found here and put on display in the museums as evidences of the pre-Christian settlements in this region.

The Derinkuyu underground city developed at the bottom of a shaft, going down 85 m. deep. There are living spaces and rooms around the shaft and a wide, peered-hall at the bottom. The wide semicircular hall was used as a meeting hall and church.

Found in Derinkuyu and on exposition in the courtyard of the Ankara Anatolian Civilizations Museum, the "Roman Eagle at the peak", a marble statue.

A passage from the Underground city.

The Ağzıkarahan Caravanserai: The monumental entrance portal is adorned with classical Seljuk decorations.

AKSARAY

The verdant town of Aksaray is located at the end of the road that turns off to Cappadocia from the main route of Ankara-Adana, and offers a rich collection of Turkish historical works. At the crossroads, there is a large new rest stop with a modern hotel, restaurant, etc. At the side of the road leading to Cappadocia from here, there are three Seljuk Turkish caravanserais, one of which is well preserved, while the remaining two are in ruins.

The 13th century Ağzıkarahan Caravanserai (Caravan Palace) is one of the best examples of old Turkish castle-lodging establishments.
Built with local stones in the classical plan, this edifice was just one of many used for caravan lodging all over the Turkish Empires.

These monumental buildings had huge entrance portals, open court yards, with galeries surrounding and central small mosques built like kiosks. The kitchen, Turkish bath and quarters of personnel are situated on the sides of the court yard. The covered sections are colossal, like a cathedral. In this section travellers could find free room and board.

The road that turns south 11 km. from Aksaray, leads to the Ihlara valley.

The Ağzıkarahan Caravanserai: The main building, north façade.

The kiosk mosque in the centre of the courtyard and the entrance to the interior section.

The Ihlara valley and the Melendiz Stream, the creator of the deep canyon.

THE IHLARA VALLEY (Peristrema)

The Ihlara valley, which completes the Cappadocian sights and tours, differs from Göreme and the Soğanlı valleys. For thousands of years, the torrential waters flowing from the Hasandağ volcano and the Melendiz mountains into the Tuz Gölü (The Salt Lake) on the Central Anatolian plain, have formed a deep canyon with myriad twists.

The slopes of the U shaped canyon are filled with large blocks of rocks that have tumbled down from successive collapses. The depth of the valley can hardly be realized unless one nears the slopes. At the bottom of the valley, the Melendiz stream furnished a source of vitality for the Christian monasteries and churches situated on the wall-like slopes. The Selime village is located on the north exit of the canyon, among the fairy chimneys at the skirts of the slope. On this slope are remnants of monastic settlements reflecting the influence of the «Syrian school».

The road following the natural course of the valley, passes the thermal baths which have been in use since the Roman period, and extends towards Hasandağı. Dominating the plateau is the Hasandağ volcano. At the end of the road, before the entrance to the Ihlara village, one takes the road turning left to enter the valley. This road leads to a modern restaurant and a rest stop. Entering the Museum area from this point, one descends by steps into the deep valley. Sixteen kilometres long, the Ihlara valley possesses more than 100 rock carved churches, along with innumerable monasteries and rooms. Recently opened to visit, the valley has a rich history and is full of archeological works and documents. Some locally-named churches are decorated with frescoes, identified to be the earliest dated in the Cappadocian region-pictured serial type, reflecting the «Syria-Egypt» influences. Some others are in the «capital style» while the late ones reveal 13th-century Turkish miniature effects. This diversity in the frescoes is evidence for the variety of origins of the monastic way of ilfe in this region. Some frescoes reflect the oriental and early-period type, with styles, symbols and legends never encountered in Byzantine art.

The facades of some churches are decorated with round vaults lined side-by-side which are Syrian in style.

The tours visit a few easily-reached frescoed churches. The Purenliseki, Karanlık, Kokar, Ağaçaltı and Sümbüllü churches are some examples of these, close to the steps going down into the valley. The names are local and attributed. Their plans show great diversity.

There is a simple-planned church, dedicated to St. George, near the Balısırma village (beside the Bahattin Samanlığı). The latest frescoes found in the region, dated from the end of the 13th century, are located here. St. George is seen between a man and a woman, dressed typically in the Turkish style of their time. The name of the Turkish Seljuk Sultan Mesud lies beside that of the Byzantine Emperor Adronicus. This offers another example of the tolerance shown the Christian subjects by the Turkish state of the time.

The northern end of the Ihlara valley, opening to the plain: The Melendiz Stream, running through a rich greenlife, reaches the plain through the canyon it has shaped. The village, Selime is situated at the foot of the table-like flat hill.

The village Selime is founded just at the foot of the fairy chimneys.

The Ihlara Valley: The view from the terrace of the restaurant overlooking the section reaching out north.

The slope descends into the Ihlara valley with steps.The southern view from the entrance panoramic terrace.

The frescoes decorating the churches of the Ihlara valley belong to different schools and are simple works of art. The Ascension of Jesus Christ to the left and the decorative frescoes on the right, belong to the Ağaçaltı Church.

The frescoes decorating the churches of the Ihlara valley has lighter colours.

KAYSERİ

Kayseri, situated on the northern skirts of the huge mass of Erciyes volcano, has been on a strategical point for centuries due to the Junction of the main roads crossing Anatolia. 20 km. east of Kayseri one of Anatolia's most important archaeological spot "Kültepe" is situated. In Kültepe where nearly the whole Hittite era is represented, precious cuneiform scripts on clay tablets giving information about that period were unearthed.

The Kayseri Archaeological Museum exhibits the findings of the vicinity in its modern construction.

Kayseri being the most important city of the region even before the Roman Era is now a developed centre of trade and industry famous for its hand-woven carpets. The nearest airport to Göreme is situated here (100 km.). The city which has been invaded by Sassanids and Arabs many times during the 8th and 9th century, literally possesses no Roman works of art. The name of the city is a Turkish adaptation of the Roman Ceasarea.

Kayseri is famous with its works from the Seljuk and Ottoman periods. Especially architecture of the 13th century, the Moslem Theological Schools, mausoleums and the Ulu Mosque are very famous.

The city walls constructed by Turks replace the Byzantine city walls. Only small parts of the outer city walls are existing.

Alaca Kümbet of the Seljuk period in Kayseri.

The historical part of the city, city centre of modern Kayseri, possesses still its characteristic colourful and live shopping atmosphere. The modern new city is spreading towards the plain.

The Huand Hatun complex constructed in 1238 is a typical example of Seljuk architecture with its mosque, Moslem Theological School, bath and mausoleum. The Döner Kümbet, The Sırçalı Kümbet and the Çifte Kümbet are the most important mausoleums.

Anatolia's biggest caravanserai Sultanhanı, constructed in 1236 is situated on the Kayseri-Sivas road.

It is also known that the master Turkish architect, Mimar Koca Sinan (Architect Sinan the Great), was born in a small village of Kayseri.

The Map of Turkey

CAPPADOCIA

BAZAAR 54

"Quality"

CARPET

- **İSTANBUL**
Nuruosmaniye Cad.
54 Cağaloğlu
Tel. (1) 511 21 50

- **İZMİR**
1373 Sok. 4/A.B.C
Alsancak
Tel. (51) 14 13 82 - 14 86.35

- **KUŞADASI**
Öküz Mehmet Paşa
Kervansarayı
Tel. (6361) 3411

- **MARMARİS**
Yat Limanı
Barbaros Cad. 1
Tel. (6121) 2786

- **BODRUM**
Neyzen Tevfik
Cad. 186/A
Tel. (6141) 2445

- **ANTALYA**
Yat Limanı Kaleiçi 4
Tel. (311) 10290

- **ASPENDOS**
Alanya Yolu.
Belkıs Harabeleri Serik
Antalya Tel. (3221) 2900

- **CAPPADOCIA**
Avanos
Zelve yolu
Tel. (4861) 1561

Bazaar 54 is an establishment of **NET GROUP of COMPANIES**

NET®
PUBLICATION LIST
- **ISTANBUL (ORT.)**
  (In English, French, German)
- **ISTANBUL (B.N.)**
  (In English, French, German, Italian, Spanish, Japanese)
- **ISTANBUL**
  (In English, French, German, Italian, Spanish, Arabic, Greek, Turkish)
- **ISTANBUL (Mini edition)**
  (In English, French, German, Italian, Spanish, Japanese, Hungarian)
- **CONTEMPORARY HANDMADE TURKISH CARPETS**
  (In English, French, German, Italian)
- **PURE SILK TURKISH CARPETS-Hereke and Kayseri**
  (In English, French, German)
- **HAGIA SOPHIA**
  (In English, French, German, Italian, Turkish)
- **THE KARİYE MUSEUM**
  (In English, French, German, Italian, Turkish)
- **THE TOPKAPI PALACE**
  (In English, French, German, Italian, Spanish, Turkish)
- **THE SACRED RELICS**
  (In English, French, German, Turkish)
- **Unique CAPPADOCIA-The Göreme Region**
  (In English, French, German, Italian, Spanish, Turkish)
- **PERGAMUM**
  (In English, French, German)
- **EPHESUS**
  (In English, French, German, Italian)
- **PAMUKKALE (HIERAPOLIS)**
  (In English, French, German, Italian, Turkish)
- **ALANYA**
  (In English, French, German, Turkish)
- **ASPENDOS**
  (In English, French, German)
- **The Capital of Urartu: VAN**
  (In English, French, German, Turkish)
- **THE SÜLEYMANİYE MOSQUE AND ITS ENVIRONMENT**
  (In English, French, German)
- **LYCIA-Western Section of the Southern Anatolian Coast**
  (In English, French, German)
- **KARIA-Western Section of the Southern Anatolian Coast**
  (In English, French, German)
- **NEMRUT (Ulgür Önen)**
  (In English, French, German)
- **VIDEO CASSETTE-Istanbul (VHS-Beta)**
  (In English, German)
- **COLOUR SLIDES** (36 different sets, 12 slides in each set)
- **THE MAPS OF TURKEY AND ISTANBUL CITY PLANS**

NET® BOOKSTORES
- **ISTANBUL,** 1. Yerebatan Caddesi, Şeftali Sokağı, 10, 34410 Cağaloğlu
  2. Ramada Hotel, Ordu Caddesi 226, 34470 Laleli
- **İZMİR,** Cumhuriyet Bulvarı, 142/B, 35210 Alsancak